FULL CIRCLE

CREATION, MIGRATION, and COMING HOME

By ELiSA BOXER
iLLUSTRATED BY VIVIAN MiNEKER

PUBLISHED BY SLEEPING BEAR PRESS™

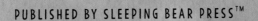

WiTH each NeW BeGiNNiNG

comes a path of possibilities—
a whole world to explore and experience.

But sometimes,
along the journey and amid the adventure
comes the powerful pull of home.

fall in Maine

The day is ending
and life is beginning.

With quick flicks of her tail,
the mother salmon digs a hole in the riverbed where she was born.
Five thousand eggs fill the nest.

Sweep
Sweep
Sweep

Her strong tail heaps gravel on top of the tiny eggs,
keeping them warm and snug
for the long winter ahead.

SPRING IN ICELAND

The day is ending
and life is beginning.

Using her beak as a bulldozer,
the mother puffin carves a cave
into the grassy cliff where she was born.

KICK
KICK
KICK

Her feet finish the job, dirt flying from the burrow until finally
it's deep enough to hold an egg.
For forty-five days, she and her mate take turns keeping it warm,
protecting it from predators.

SPRING IN the GULF of MeXiCO

The day is ending
and life is beginning.
The mother bluefin tuna makes millions of tiny eggs that . . .

. . . float
float
float . . .

. . . in the warm waters where she was born,
in the dark of night
when fewer predators are awake.
Still, only two of those eggs
will survive.

SUMMER IN COSTA RICA

The day is ending
and life is beginning.

Using her back flippers as shovels,
the mother sea turtle digs a ditch in the soft sand where she was born.
One hundred eggs fill the nest.

SCOOP
SCOOP
SCOOP

Her front flippers heap sand in the hole
to hide the eggs from predators.
Her nest now concealed,
she crawls out to sea.

She's hatching!

The baby salmon breaks free.
Brown with vertical stripes,
she's camouflaged among the reeds in the river.

As she grows, she swims out to sea,

dodging double-crested cormorants with wings spread, waiting to scoop up dinner.

The salmon turns silver like the water so she's not easily spotted by hungry seals resting on rocky ridges.

She's hatching!

A baby puffin, fluffy and black.
For weeks, her parents bring beakfuls of fish into the burrow.

When she's strong enough to leave the nest,
she hobbles along the rocky cliff
and takes flight, soaring out to sea.

In the open ocean, powerful thrusts of her feet propel her along the surface.

A gull circling overhead sees his next meal. He sets up to dive bomb, but the puffin's feathers are black, so he keeps losing sight of her against the dark sea.

She's hatching!

After only two days, the hungry baby bluefin tuna breaks free.
She grows quickly, seeking out meals of mackerel and eels.
When her sharp vision spots a squid,
she can dive down half a mile to catch and devour it.
Shaped like a torpedo, she's one of the ocean's fastest fish,
and she needs that speed to avoid orcas.

Her dark blue top and silver bottom blend with the shimmering sea,
but fishermen are on the hunt with their rods, reels, and nets.

She's hatchiNG!

The tiny sea turtle
uses her temporary tooth to emerge.
Under cover of night,
following the reflection of the moon
on the surface of the sea,
she runs across the sand from hungry gulls and human poachers.

As she matures and migrates,
she thwarts tiger sharks sneaking up from the depths
and trawlers trapping everything in their path.

SeveRaL yeaRS aND thousaNDS of Miles away

Somewhere inside, the salmon knows it's time.
She turns around.
Following the stars, the smells, and her sense of the sea,
she retraces her journey.

SeveRaL YeaRS aND thouSaNDS of MiLES away

Somewhere inside, the puffin knows it's time.
She turns around.
Following the stars, the smells, and her sense of the sea,
she retraces her journey.

SEVERAL YEARS AND thOUSANDS of MILES away

Somewhere inside, the bluefin tuna knows it's time.
She turns around.

Following the stars, the smells, and her sense of the sea,
she retraces her journey.

SEVERAL YEARS AND THOUSANDS OF MILES away

Somewhere inside, the sea turtle knows it's time.
She turns around.

Following the stars, the smells, and her sense of the sea,
she retraces her journey.

and the stream whispers . . .

aND the Cliff WhiSPeRS . . .

AND the SAND WHISPERS . . .

welcome home

welcome home

welcome home

welcome home

author's note

Growing up on the Maine coast, where there have been long-standing efforts to restore dwindling salmon populations, I was always fascinated by stories of Atlantic salmon traveling thousands of miles away to Greenland and then somehow managing to find their way back home to the exact spot where they hatched.

Later, I learned that other animals also have this remarkable ability. Natal homing—also known as natal philopatry—is a phenomenon mostly seen in sea birds like puffins and sea animals like turtles, salmon, and bluefin tuna.

When it's time to start families of their own, that's when they come home.

No one knows exactly how these creatures manage to find their way back after migrating thousands of miles out to sea. It's a miraculous mystery. Some scientists believe they use the earth's magnetic field as a kind of compass. Others say they are guided back home by the tastes, sounds, or smells of the ocean. Still others believe the animals follow the stars. So there are multiple theories, but no clear answers, as to how exactly these animals manage to find their way back to the exact spot where they were born after traveling such great distances.

This topic hits close to home for me.

After landing my first job in Boston, then moving to New York for graduate school, I eventually found my way back to Maine, to raise my family.

When I began researching this book, I described it to my son. He asked: "If they're going to end up where they started anyway, why do they leave?"

Good question, right?

Whatever journey we're on, maybe we need to go through experiences that test us, challenges that shape us, and situations that help us define who we are, and who we are not.

So, in the end, we can return to who we were all along, honed by everything we've been through.

In other words, without going away, there's no coming home.

atlantic Salmon

- ▶ They can jump almost 12 feet high.
- ▶ They stop eating once they come back to fresh water to spawn, and can live off their body fat for more than a year.
- ▶ The biggest one caught in North America weighed 55 pounds.
- ▶ Their age can be determined by the number of rings inside their ears.

! PREDATORS
Sea Birds, Tuna, Seals, and Bears

Puffins

- ▶ Their beaks change color. Just before winter, they shed their bright orange bill, and underneath is a pale grey one.
- ▶ The female lays only one egg at a time.
- ▶ Using their wings to "fly" underwater and their feet to steer, they can dive up to 60 meters down.
- ▶ They're one of the few birds that can carry multiple fish in their beak—up to ten at a time.

! PREDATORS
Gulls, Hawks, Seals, and Fox

Bluefin tuna

- ▶ They need to keep swimming in order to breathe.
- ▶ They are one of the world's most critically endangered species.
- ▶ Each tuna can lay up to 540 million eggs in one season.
- ▶ Bluefin is a delicacy in Asia, where one fish sold for $1.7 million in 2013.

! PReDatoRS
Sharks, Whales, and Recreational and Commercial Fishermen

Sea turtles

- ▶ They can live to be 150 years old, although most live to be around 50.
- ▶ They can't retract their heads or flippers into their shells like other turtles.
- ▶ Nearly all seven species are classified as endangered.
- ▶ The species have been around since the time of the dinosaurs—around 110 million years.

! PReDatoRS
Vultures, Crabs, Sharks, Fishing Nets, and Plastic

For Andy, Owen, Louie and Daphne. Welcome home.

—Elisa

To Darlie, who will always be a part of me.

—Vivian

The author gratefully acknowledges the time and expertise of Dr. Walt Golet, assistant professor in the
School of Marine Sciences at the University of Maine and the Gulf of Maine Research Institute.

SLEEPING BEAR PRESS™

2395 South Huron Parkway, Suite 200, Ann Arbor, MI 48104
www.sleepingbearpress.com © Sleeping Bear Press

Printed and bound in the United States
10 9 8 7 6 5 4 3 2 1

Library of Congress Cataloging-in-Publication Data
Names: Boxer, Elisa, author. | Mineker, Vivian, illustrator.
Title: Full circle : creation, migration, and coming home / written by
Elisa Boxer ; illustrated by Vivian Mineker.
Description: Ann Arbor, MI : Sleeping Bear Press, [2024] | Audience: Ages
4-8 | Summary: "This lyrical adventure follows the bluefin tuna, puffin,
sea turtle, and Atlantic salmon through their life cycle. Each of these
special species has a characteristic called natal homing. They're born,
leave home to eat and mate, and then return to precisely where they were
born to start their own families"-- Provided by publisher.
Identifiers: LCCN 2024007716 | ISBN 9781534112810 (hardcover)
Subjects: LCSH: Life cycles (Biology)--Juvenile literature. | Animal
migration--Juvenile literature. | Biological rhythms--Juvenile
literature. | Parturition grounds--Juvenile literature.
Classification: LCC QH501 .B724 2024 | DDC 591.56--dc23/eng/20240317
LC record available at https://lccn.loc.gov/2024007716

Photos: Ghost Crab: M.E. Parker/Shutterstock.com, American Black Vulture: Sunshower Shots/Shutterstock.com, Arctic Fox: Cecilie Bergan Stuedal/Shutterstock.com,
Puffin: Summit Art Creations/Shutterstock.com, Salmon: Paul Abrahams/Shutterstock.com, Beach Pollution: Kochneva Tetyana/Shutterstock.com, Black Bear: Ben McMurtray/Shutterstock.com,
Bluefin Tuna: lunamarina/Shutterstock.com, Harris Hawk: acceptphoto/Shutterstock.com, Commercial Fisherman: Josep Curto/Shutterstock.com, Sea Turtle: idreamphoto/Shutterstock.com,
Orca Whale: Tory Kallman/Shutterstock.com, Northern Gannet: Jesus Cobaleda/Shutterstock.com, Great White Shark: LuckyStep/Shutterstock.com, Black Backed Gull: Motalb/Shutterstock.com,
Seal: Enessa Varnaeva/Shutterstock.com, Recreational Fisherman: Maridav/Shutterstock.com